97 SMILES

She knew, as she stepped from the train, this had been the wrong decision. She succumbed to his embrace but that love feeling didn't burst from her stomach. It was flat. He stepped back to admire her and she smelled stale cigarettes under mint … the cigarettes he'd vowed he'd given up.

She was pleased she'd come for how else would she know, at home, surrounded by indecision?

Only by stepping out, taking a chance, did she know for sure. Buying a return ticket she felt his sadness and none of hers – only relief at clarity's arrival.

Philip J Bradbury

97 Special Moments In Life's Exquisite Simplicity

Philip J Bradbury

The 53 words hadn't meant to go for a walk. They really hadn't. Their parent, the writer, when questioned, couldn't quite explain their emergence either. So, here they were, walking about in plain daylight with no idea of what to do or where to go and their writer wasn't of any help at all. No one would take them in, give them a book to live in, so they continued wandering while their writer let them freeze while he gave birth to another 53 words. Then another 53 words. Every day another 53 words he produced and still no book or publisher would let them in.

When pressed he admitted to birthing the 53 words "just because I enjoy it."

"That sounds a bit thoughtless, a bit callous," we suggested.

"I'd never thought about it like that," he countered.

"So what started them?"

"It was a Flash Fiction contest here in Brisbane."

"Flash Fiction?"

"Exactly," he said. "I'd never heard of it either. It turned out it means very short stories and this competition was for stories under a hundred words."

"So you won it?"

"Not likely!" he said, laughing. "I'd submitted two stories which probably came last … certainly not winners. However, I'd had so much fun writing these stories I decided not to let them go, to do something with them."

"And you did what?"

"Nothing. I left that question to my muses and, three days later, they suggested I write 53 53-word stories. One a day. I relished the challenge and enjoyed the writing."

"Why 53?"

"Don't know. Just liked the number, I guess. Then, a few weeks later, remembered I was born in 1953 … who knows why 53. I just liked the number."

"So you've set these 53 stories free, sent them out into a cold, uncaring world without a warm book to live in, to uplift people. How's that feel?"

Horrible, really. I've tried to find publishers but no one's interested. I feel like I've given birth to orphans and I don't know how to find a home for the. I feel like I've abandoned them. Sad, really …"

And then the silly sod decides to write 97 97-word stories ... ho hum!

What readers are saying about this book ...

This work is brilliant. It is darker than the 53 SMILES but it is thought provoking to the reader and causes them to question what is happening for them. Sometimes it gives the answer to the question and sometimes it doesn't. The wording is poetic and beautifully written. This book is best delved into rather than being read from cover to cover and is less about being entertained and more about being challenged to grow personally. The writer shows understanding and maturity."

~ *Anna Louise, life coach at www.annalouiselifecoaching.com*

The master of *A Course In Miracles* tells us that we are "Moving to a place beyond words on a journey without distance to a place we never left." He's literally helping us to "roll away the stone."

In his book *97 Smiles*, Philip J Bradbury is utilizing the era of less is more. He's actually assisting us to cut our addiction to story by giving us just enough words to provoke a question or two. The tightly packed stories invoke more stillness and time to ponder, "And then what?" Illusions of despair and comfort may seem to come and go, but behind each story there is reality, there is God. Philip cleverly shows us our hidden fear of God by exposing our tendency to dive deep into fantasy whilst hardly daring to dip our toe in the waters of reality.

I think congratulations are in order Mr Bradbury. I am looking forward to your account of what can happen when we drop the shackles of fantasy and dive headlong into God.

~*Sallyann Gaelic, Writer and Teacher*

Wind rushes through and the trees change, losing their leaves. Growing stronger. And so must we.

Raising the winds of hope must incur an equal and opposite fall to the doldrums ... unless there's a bending and a loss.

Changing a relationship, job or location means letting go of that which angered us before. Otherwise, we marry another body but same person; another location, same neighbourhood.

Hoping for love without removing the blocks to love will ensure the zephyrs of hopelessness turn to an icy storm, chilling a fragile soul.

There is always letting go before attaining.

Arnox was as big as a skip, mean as a buzzard and happily cracked sculls.

His woman, blonde and blingy, cracked walnuts between her knees and picked up coins with her labia. Though men paid for her nightly onstage nakedness, she was exclusively Arnox's. Arnox, however, didn't return exclusivity; he roamed and played every toe-curler offered … and many that weren't.

Every mountain has a crack and Arnox's was his mum. She'd taught him manipulation from birth, round her gnarly finger. Mess with her and Arnox'll have your cracked scull in t'skip.

We're all exclusive to someone.

He leapt from his horse; guns a'blazing, his mouth dry and heart pounding. He skittered behind a hedge, towing his horse. He looked through the gaps, saw nothing, and the deathly silence filled him with dread. He assessed his

chances as his horse stood there quaking, it's trusting button eyes looking at him, waiting for his next move.

Not the first time and he cursed his slow reactions. They'd be upon him soon if he didn't make a sure move ...

"Dinner's ready, boys!" yelled his mother.

He smiled, leapt up and towed his wooden horse inside.

Transcendent peace besets, upsets and regrets us. Retaining contentment every moment, no matter our circumstances, is a driver with subtle relentlessness.

We choose misery and anger, hoping they offer something … as a poor substitute for that deeper longing; the deeper longing to forget the world's angst and to be noticed by God. We buy our toys and accolades, hoping the peace will come. It doesn't so we buy more.

Amassing more of the transient world the deep, abiding peace watches us as a parent watches a wilful child. Always there, it wishes constantly for our return.

She teetered on the brink, about to end it all, when her mother called, "Can you go to the shop please? And Burok's here. Take him along." She left with a scowl and a boy and returned with a smile and a man.

She wondered at life's delicate balance – saved by a mother's request; a boy's interest.

Or was God answering every call for love? A last minute answer that always came.

She hugged her son and smiled at her husband, Burok. She only knew and cared that she was back from the brink, safer now ... perhaps.

In existence lived below the spark, there's silent desperation.

This sparkless drudgery, maskerading as life, stifles a desire we think we cannot fulfil. This desire, this ancient warmth, glows in silent remembrance.

Instead, we heap upon it the dead ashes of oughtism, of shouldism, based on a guilt never eased. We succumb to pedantry when we might fly. We wonder why earth sucks and our bones ache.

Our spark ever glows as we smother it. It glows beneath the dead ashes, drowned in fear. It could, instead, take us to potential beyond imagination ... take us home.

If ever the stage was made for one, 'twas for Byron Perfidy's strut and sonorous voice. Mirrors, darlings, were not for vanity. They assured perfection for public enjoyment.

A dramatic line was perfectly controlled but not the six-year drought or the government, bankrupting the country of money and spirit. People thirsted for food of body and soul and opened to the Justice Church, preaching damnation and modesty, banning happiness and mirrors.

Byron had two choices and took the offensive, becoming JC's most ardent performer, the only man in town with a mirror in his exclusive apartment.

Gullick hated beaches with a vengeance.

With the warm sun and gentle breezes, the swarms of prattling people arriving with their screaming kids, wild games, noisy radios. His own family argued over food and space.

Then, in the summer's heat, the pristine sand would be covered by fat, scalding, greasy bodies, comatose and flaccid.

Later, the winter's slash would drive them all away. The wet sand would bounce morosely as it was beaten by the wild hail and it was miserably lonely. Too lonely.

As he rose, he wished he'd been born an eagle, not a seagull.

There's a balm we pour across our rough and troubled world; words of plaster to fill our cracked and ragged lives.

Elephants in the room feed voraciously on these pretences of peace, growing to crowd out our creativity and peace.

We might, instead, speak the words of our lonely despair, our guilty secrets.

We might, in sinless clarity, release the demons through our mouths, burning our throats and cleansing our souls.

The more we hide, the more we fear, till it consumes us.

Alternatively, the more we release, the more we are released – expansion in the freedom.

Sargent O'Brien towed his men over the last hill (he hoped), his rasping voice hauling guts and pride, the men dragging packs and SLR rifles under Turkish sun. Two weeks hiding and marching, no food, little water, limbs dead. Only loyalty and comradeship were left to fire up adrenalin.

Cresting the rise, expecting enemy fire, they saw the pristine uniform of Lieutenant MacGuire.

"The war's been over a week, dummys," she laughed.

They saw red as did the white uniform, quickly slumped to the ground.

Our faintest enemy is authority's plea; humiliation's command is our fiercest foe.

Aside from the little I tell myself, there is less and less I listen to.

Politicians tell me, "You can trust me," (which I surely can't), salesmen tell me, "It's new and improved," (which is an impossibility) and most others bombard me with their opinions.

Opinions are mush from the uninformed. They change by day, by mood, by place and by the company they keep. People are enraged by others' words; they're so infantile they'll allow someone's transient and changing opinion shape their view of themselves.

I choose the wisdom of silence over hot air and noise.

Timmy cowered from insults and punches of Pauly's group; the perfect target with glasses, buck teeth and skinny legs.

With neither strength nor mind for fighting back, he lived in constant fear, imagining (hoping) his body being found one morning. His misery'd be over.

Then something happened.

They were beating a new, scrawnier boy. A mind-door opened and out stepped Superman; a larger version of himself not seen before. Standing for fairness, careless of consequences, Superman flew into the melee, scattering bully boys. They faltered, then ran.

A mind switch and hero to all, Timid became Timpestuous.

He took his ageing body to the sea – as he'd done for forty years – and smiled as he eased into the welcoming waves. His frail arms and legs became powerful propellants in the weightlessness of water. He strode out horizontally from the shore.

Despite annual shark attacks and drownings, he'd somehow glided through every peril, as though invisible.

He preferred drowning in the cool, caring sea than family's fussing concerns and restraints.

The jet ski bumped and carried on as a contented soul released its body and swam into that larger sea of consciousness; now totally free.

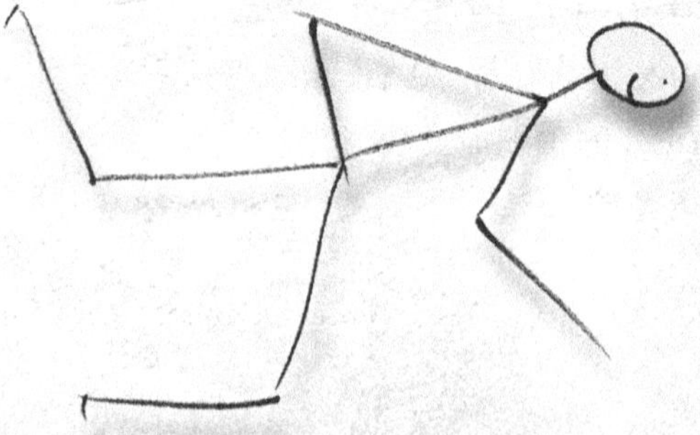

The key in his back, wound each day by duty and habit, turned relentlessly.

The rising sun's welcome drew up the curtain of dew, revealing bowed maize, glistening trees, chattering birds. He saw only paperwork, never complete. Daily the key, not he, drove him forward.

Then the key fell out. He rose and, strangely, woke up. The yellow maize and sighing trees filled him. He cried as bird song stroked his aching heart and recalled an ancient song long forgotten.

He learned to teach. Some called it breakdown. He called it break-in. His pupils called him breakthrough.

Easier getting fish to walk than getting Gordon to like towns. Raising sheep, cattle and wheat was what he knew and did well; Friday nights drinking with his mates and Saturday playing rugby. With his best friends, his dogs, he prospered, despite droughts, economic downturns and diseases.

Nearly got a girlfriend, once.

A farm with a mine's like a fish with feet; just not right. Despite the mining company's huge offers, Gordon kept saying no. The police took him away to his government/mining funded town house. He died soon after; a fish sadly panting in the dirt.

If it wasn't the right colour, shape or brand, he'd scream till his parents rushed to bring the right gift … and their guilt.

Angry demanding worked as a child so he continue to blame and scream at the world for its wrongs on him.

He lost friends and jobs and yelled at his parents for not bringing him up better. All they could bring him now was their guilt … and the lesson that all the wrongs were others' fault.

He then become a policeman where the law backed his petty needs … and anger remained.

I cricked my neck against the irritation of my new suit, hoping it would ease. This was going to be one long party.

I looked back at my sleek new vehicle. It was the fastest I'd ever driven; the fastest anyone had ever driven.

The massive space between Kathy and I would be gone soon. She'd soon be here. I thought about the folks back home and the ones who'd be arriving soon and smiled.

I was proud of my choices – Kathy, friends, career – and that I'd become the first man to arrive and live on Mars.

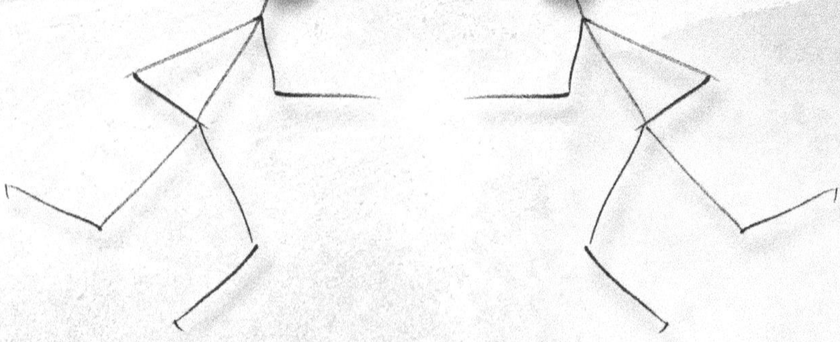

As I returned toward the shore, after many tides away, I saw them. Again. Still.

The flashing, churning limbs of those land creatures never go away. Always in our water. Always forgetting our warnings and requests.

They come from the land, seeking to rule (no, destroy), killing us and our food with hooks and nets and poisoning our homesea.

We're not hungry or stupid; just desperate and communicating. We just want them to stay on their land like we stay in our water. We scare them but do they listen? How else can we say, "Enough," please? [2]

Gerald wasn't like other gulls. He had a particular affinity for being where he didn't intend to be: tangled in trees, slammed into lamp posts or plonking into swimming pools. An embarrassment to others, he found himself more and more alone … and sad.

Then he crashed through the window of Christopher, a lonely rich boy. Christopher tended his wounds, fed him and was then provided endless entertainment with Gerald's clumsy antics. Gerald could give up flying's dangers as they became lifelong chums.

Love is blind but never stupid, always finding ways to complete the jigsaw of happiness.

I dived in and soon found myself sucked out too far and too tired to swim back against the current.

Exhausted, I stopped thrashing and called my friend (God) for help. I immediately sensed my layers: one layer was exhausted, breathless, panicked and afraid of dying; the other was peaceful and assured.

I chose to act on the second layer's still, quiet voice: I lay on my back and quietly kicked. Imperceptibly I inched towards the beach and then landed safely, grateful to be reunited with dry land.

"All calls to Truth are answered with a miracle."(3)

The frothing, screaming vortex we're in is as real and turbulent as we wish it to be. We call it our world, our life and we cherish it dearly.

There is a tiny, golden moment we reach when we've had enough. This moment isn't reached by denial but by immersion – by feeling fully the depth of despair and anger, by diving to the murky bottom, holding the pain and then releasing it.

Our holding and releasing gives us release and hold to a new, clean and simple stillness we crave, when drama and pain are fully uncherished.

Christmas is the toughest time of the year for many, many people.

"The Season" expects us to be happy and to be surrounded by friends and family. Many of us don't have family and friends. In the face of society's pressure to be otherwise, the feelings of loneliness and not-fitting-in arise like an exploding Christmas cracker. For these people, there's none to turn to, to tell the loneliness to.

The Christ is reborn in us every time we reach out to one of these lonesome souls and every time we listen and hear their pain. That's Christmiss-ion.

Our stories are born of a future memory at birth. They ache to grow and nourish all around them, thirsting for new words and pages each day.

Smiles add new words, kindness adds paragraphs, risking love adds pages.

Each subjugation of spirit rips out chapters, acting small burns paper, people-pleasing fades ink.

Our choices, then, are not about doing the right thing but about being gracious bearers of story-lines to those who've stumbled short; being loving warriors with fiery pens, holding others' words and pages when they fall and forget.

Bind your life loosely, let it grow.

The salt of yesterday taints my food and it's rancid, cloyingly familiar.

You smile and it's *that* look my mother gave me, as a child; I feel shamed. You compliment me and it's *that* phrase my father always used; I feel angry.

My body is here today but my mind sees it in yesterday's mirrors.

I must let in the undiluted past, squarely accept, forgive and release it. I let it return to where it belongs ... in the past.

Only then can I live in the freshness of this sacred moment, taste this sweet and juicy aliveness.

Albert chose to impose his own narrative on the world around him.

He saw black where there was grey; experienced rage when there was annoyance; heard commands when there were questions.

The witnesses to his narrative appeared, daily, justifying his views. His bones felt mammoth-like – large, heavy and inflexible – and his life was heavier, slower.

Then, one day, it was all too heavy. He gave up needing to know ... not not-caring but not-knowing.

Greys turned to white, annoyances to so-what and questions remained questions. His bones became young and his wisdom ageless. Albert smiled at last.

If he hadn't decided, just because, to take a different route home ... if he hadn't tripped on a kerb, next to an old school friend ... if he hadn't accepted a drink from said school chum ... if he hadn't been late home to a suspicious fiancé ... if Mary hadn't dumped him ... if he hadn't been sitting at the cliff top, contemplating suicide ... if he hadn't been robbed at the cliff top ... if he hadn't made an insurance claim for said robbery, he wouldn't have met Josephine, the love of his life.

Jasmine heard we should divert Sydney's New Year fireworks money to starving farmers; divert UK's foreign aid to Yorkshire's flood victims; imprison some people, forgive others. Governments should do this, teachers do that, police do this, neighbours do that.

Opinions blowing in her face like confetti at a windy wedding; beautiful and useless.

She smiled, thinking how loose our lives are, like the tired skin on a dying elephant; the tusks (our truths) enveloped in the shifting sands.

Opinions, the last bastion of a frightened and inconsequential world ... in her opinion anyway!

And another elephant dies.

Emanuel wondered how the world's organisers left mayhem in their wake.

Politicians promised us peace and led us to war. Economists promised prosperity and stole from paupers. Police promised protection and shot innocents. Doctors promised health while inoculating with poisons.

"The more we're placated, the more we're disturbed," he said, my fear rising.

"Disorganisation's bad ..." I whimpered.

"So, stop doing what makes it badder!" he implored. "The world's fine, we're fine. Leave us alone!"

He scared me – my life's disorganisation meant I had to control others ... or sort me out.

I feared that the most.

Charmaine asked, "If you could be anything, what would it be?"

"I … don't know," I said. Fear sucked my bones.

"Yes you do. What would it be?"

"Unsure." Fear sucked at my stomach.

"What do you dream of?"

"I don't," I said, lying badly.

"You do," she said kindly, my secrets bared.

"Actually, a writer." Fear sucked my brain.

"Saying it brings fear of failure. Suck failure in."

I couldn't resist her and sucked. None came. It was empty. I was empty.

"Suck in *writer*. How's that feel?"

"Full. Complete," I said. A gentle fire blew.

Quietly, desperately, I said, "I need to understand,"

"Like you need to understand engines before you drive?" Ben asked.

"That's different. I need to understand life."

"Like you need to understand physiology before you have sex?" he asked, with a tiny smile.

"That's different. Life is different. I need to understand it."

"Unlike the zillions of people who have survived it without understanding it?"

"That's not fair."

"And the zillions who understood life and still died?"

"Right, why do I need to understand, then?"

"To pretend that the illusion of knowledge is grander than peace and happiness."

In the hidden folds of our lives are dreams we stashed away and soon forgot … the dragons we'd slay, maidens we'd save, how many stars we'd visit, what we'd do as ruler of the world, how many books we'd write or records we'd break.

"Where did our dreams go?" we ask, when we start to grow up. Then, when we've grown up, we forget the question and the secrets. There's just *ought to* and *should* to battle with as the folds are ironed out, just like all the neighbours.

Dreamers ought to and should grow up!

Safe in the arms of needless activity, Nancy skittered about the planet serving the impression she thought she had on others. Short on concentration and long on promises – both unfulfilled – she feared, most of all, to look into and beyond her tired eyes.

At a quickening pace she gathered more toys, fleeting friends and conversations on things she couldn't change – politics, weather, starlets' affairs and neighbours' pettiness.

They said it was safe – and even satisfying – to find stillness and silence but the risk was too much.

She died at 53 with a broken heart and nothing achieved.

Harold was a battle hardened veteran and left, yet again, to defend his master's territory.

This time, his attackers were too numerous and strong and they left him, bleeding, in the dry grass of a farmer's field. Two days later, as he was starting to recover, a farm vehicle ran over him, breaking bones and internal organs.

Harold was, however, a fighter and dragged himself back home, four days after leaving, starved and dying.

When we saw him at the front door we took him to the vet, had him put down and we got another cat.

The bible says that Adam fell into a deep sleep. Nowhere, however, does it mention that he woke up.[4]

We ride off on our nightmares, chasing dreams, vanquishing and changing the world ... making it better. We are impassioned, ruthless and tireless.

Then, as the leaves of time turn brown and fall, it dawns on us that the world changed not one iota from our valiant, sustained efforts.

Then, as more leaves fall from our eyes, we realise we're still asleep. In fact, the whole world's a dream, masquerading as our reality.

None of it matters. Ever.

As the fingers of time draw us inexorably forward, we have but two choices:

Firstly, we can resist and sit as an old cheese, growing rancid and brittle on the shelf.

Or, secondly, we can flow as soft, sweet cream over strawberries, exploring every unexpected crevice and bump on the way.

Either way we'll be consumed and gone:

Firstly, by creeping mould and scurrying vermin, forgotten forever.

Or, secondly, by the soft, happy lips of children to be remembered for a day, a month or a life-time.

We need only make the choice: to flow or no.

As the dance-crazed wind raged about her feet, at life's precipice, she held firm, watching others leap, falter, plunge and, eventually, parachutes opening as they glided to safety. Some parachutes turned to wings and they soared off.

"Your parachute won't open till you jump," he said.

She'd jumped before – left home, hitch-hiked the world, had jobs and relationships. But, this time, she couldn't leave her abusive relationship.

"How's abuse serving you? You need pity, attention, drama?"

"My last partner committed suicide when I left."

"The past *colours* but doesn't *determine* your future."

She jumped; guilt-free, and flew.

Mac rose with the sun, uncollared and freed his scampering dog and collared the horse, ploughing the home field before the tax man arrived.

The bureaucrat danced warily between mud puddles, his pretty shoes soon dirty. His collar was tighter and his chain (tie) was shorter than the dog's and his tight suit allowed no arm raising or jolliness.

"Legally, we must keep our accounts in English and in legible order?" Mac asked.

"Yes," said the inspector, wincing.

"They're legally filed in the effluent pit there, under twenty feet of cow shit."

The tax man never returned.[5]

We grew up together, all in the same body.

There's Bombastic Bill, Victim Vera, Sultry Sue, Timid Tina and Cheeky Charlice. The body, the "person" others see, is Miranda Jacobs.

Miranda the child and teenager was awed by us, terrified she was mad. But Miranda the adult is finding acceptance and taking charge. She's realised she can be bad, a cad, sad, glad and had but she's not mad.

Mad is for the white-coated, degree-festooned ones who fear diversity, spontaneity and uncontrollability. Mad is pretending singularity while Miranda revels in her juicy diversity, like other normal people.

As we chugged round the estuary, searching for the perfect fishing spot, Eric said, "Every Viking needs their boat."

Every fisherman's an expert and eight blokes had eight different perfect spots; all devoid of fish. As we looked at who or what to blame – bait, weather, skipper, tide, stars, God – my feet felt wet ... then my ankles and I realised we were going downhill towards those elusive fish.

An avalanche of humans crashed towards the stern and the boat looked up again.

Vikings forgot every quarrel, happy to be alive!

Big fish (problems) swallowed little fish.[6]

The rabbit doesn't have to run faster than the fox; only faster than another rabbit.

Similarly, experts are those who know something at least five minutes before you do. You learn and you're an expert – the partner-changing dance of knowledge.

An expert knows things from when they experienced them; champions of telling you what you should have done yesterday. Their special function: past masters.

An expert gives perfect solutions, coloured by their past. An innocent – a blinkers-off, know-nothing – cannot screen out unimagined possibilities.

The expert is the fastest rabbit; the innocent is the fox, creating new futures.

What's the meaning of life … of *your* life in particular?

The secret to the meaning of life is that there is no secret – life has no meaning, none whatsoever.

You are a crystal bowl among seven billion other crystal bowls. You put fruit in the bowl and call yourself a fruit bowl. You put sweets in and call yourself a sweets bowl. Your life is empty and meaningless … until you decide to fill it with something you find meaningful.

That, my friend, is the meaning of your life – what you fill you with.

Your choice.

Jerry seethed. "What the hell do ya mean *I should step back a space from my own personality*?" he demanded.

"Create a space and look down on your angry self," she suggested carefully.

"I'm not bloody angry!"

"We're never angry for the reasons we think[7]," she said, evenly.

"I'm angry 'cause you piss me off!"

"You want to give me that much power over you? I thought you were stronger than that," she said, bravely.

"Smart arse!"

"Do you want to take back that control?"

"So you can be bloody right?"

"So you can find peace."

"Humph!"

Trees stood and did nothing. The magpies landed and quietly surveyed the scuttling humans about their ever-so-important business.

Humans made wars, love, money, poverty, friends and enemies in their constant quest to make a difference. Humans did much and nothing changed. They still fought, argued, judged and wept.

Sap rose, buds sprouted and leaves sighed themselves open, giving food and homes to birds. Roots eased through rocky hardness and tickled the earth, exciting worms and a million other crawly beasts. Grass was sheltered, nurturing animals and insects.

The do-nothing trees made much that was not there before.

Stephen waited forty years for his dreams to sprout.

Then, cautiously, he asked his son about his success and his own lack of same.

"The giant bamboo grows thirty metres high," his son said. "For the first five years, we see nothing above the ground but the farmer still waters it every day. Then, in the fifth year, it shoots to the sky."

"So what?" asked Stephen, confused.

"If the farmer doesn't water it every day, there's no bamboo. How much watering – not dreaming but action – have you taken towards your dreams sprouting?"

A life wasted dreaming.

"Pardon?" I asked, annoyed by his intrusion.

"Lemmings, beginnings and endings run together. I was made redundant the same month my wife demanded a divorce and I was diagnosed with cancer. End of my job, marriage and health. Then I was cleared of cancer the same month my grandchild was born and my business had its first $100,000 sales month."

"Your wife had second thoughts, perhaps?"

"She left a loser for a bigger loser, now bankrupt, and my previous employer was liquidated."

"Like attracts like," I said, happy for his blunt intrusion ... his success could rub off.

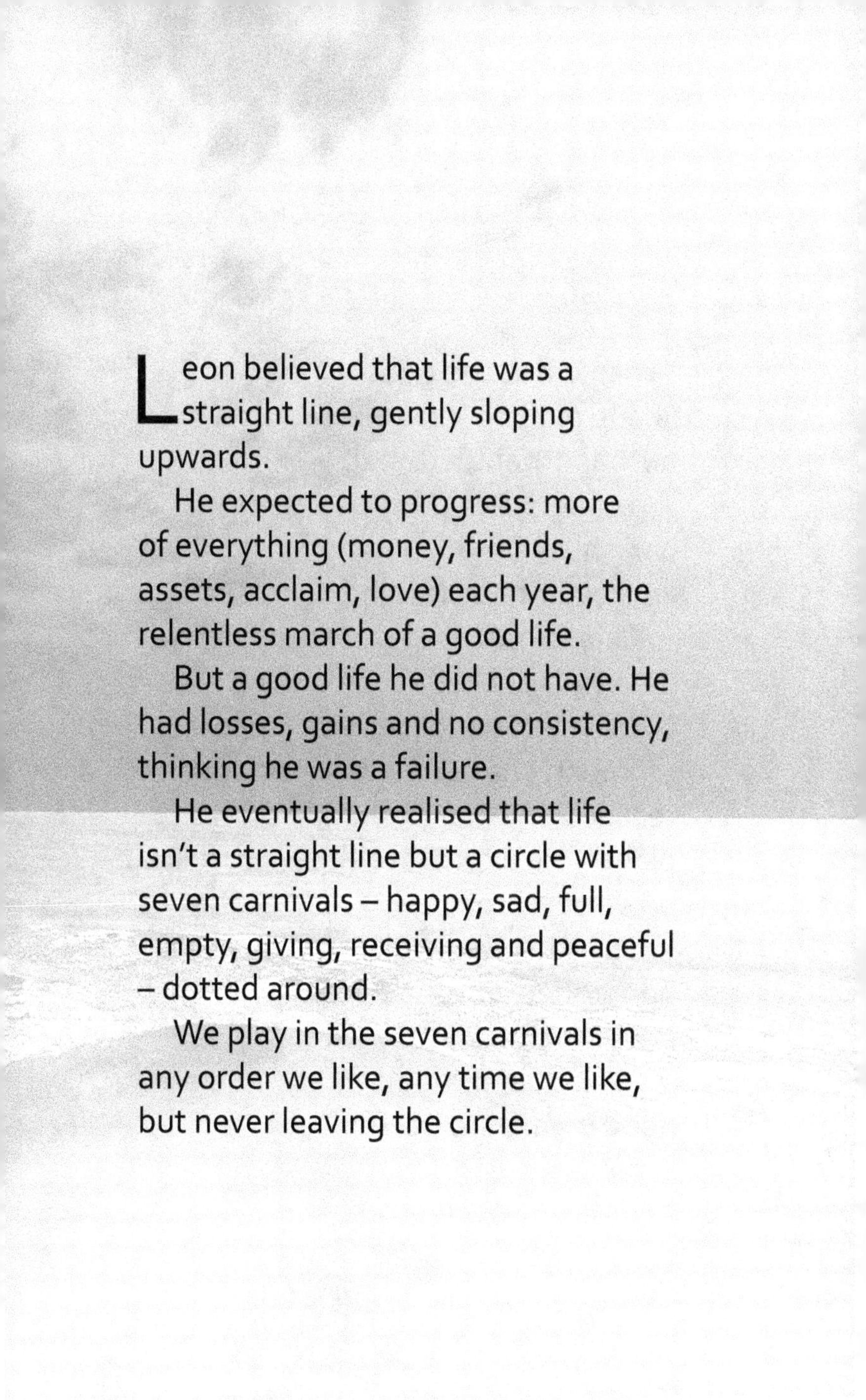

Leon believed that life was a straight line, gently sloping upwards.

He expected to progress: more of everything (money, friends, assets, acclaim, love) each year, the relentless march of a good life.

But a good life he did not have. He had losses, gains and no consistency, thinking he was a failure.

He eventually realised that life isn't a straight line but a circle with seven carnivals – happy, sad, full, empty, giving, receiving and peaceful – dotted around.

We play in the seven carnivals in any order we like, any time we like, but never leaving the circle.

Joanie was the good wife, obedient and giving. What else would a husband want, after all?

Though the affairs nearly killed her, she hung on, hoping for improvement. Nothing improved.

The divorce sent her reeling into a cess-pit of despair and nobody could reach her till, at the deepest moment, she reached herself and recalled how her husband flew his planes. He'd turn into the wind, full power, and soar.

She took that which was against her, turned it around and had it lift her up.

No longer a "good wife", she's a good woman to herself.

Woolyum the sheep asked, "Why's he poison the grass with that spray?"

"To kill the grass grubs," said Neighthan the horse, sadly.

"We only arrive to warn him that the poisonous fertilizer is killing the worms," said the grass grubs together, in four-part harmony.

"Without us, the soil dies and so does his grass," said Wormald, the last worm in the paddock.

"Can we get him to understand the damage he's causing?" asked Booven the cow.

"We can't," said Neighthan, sadly. "He thinks nothing's his fault."

"The stupidity and self-harm of the arrogant!" said Woolyum, smiling glumly.

Suicide questions seldom visit methods. Normally, they're on leaving and arriving:

"How to leave this callous, demanding and insane world I don't fit?" and, "How to come home to that accepting, peaceful and simple place I've never been to but an ancient memory says I have?"

It's the *not being here and being there* and, most often, I imagine staying alive – sneak out, invent a new identity and start again, somehow.

Sometimes opportunity's there and another body's found. Usually, however, a live pretender lurks behind a falsely smiling face, desperately wanting out.

Maybe everyone's contemplating escape ...

Joey smiled and sighed: "It was such a freedom to have the cell door slam behind me."

"Freedom?" I asked, astounded. "You're in prison!"

"But these bars are solid. I can touch them," he said. "The verbal bars are of her abuse were invisible. I couldn't deal with them. No one could see them and no one would help."

"But you're a murderer."

"Aye, a murderer of her body," he said, nodding. "But not a murderer of her spirit though. What's the greater crime?"

"Yours was killed every day?"

"Now it's free. And you've come to help."

Turtle was resting on a rock when Turtle Dove landed by his face.

"Hey, Turt, are we related?" asked Dove, chipper and chatty.

"No and don't call me Turt," said Turtle, slowly, drily.

"Grumpy!"

"Bug off. Give me peace," said Turtle, wearily.

"I am peace!" squeaked Dove. "I found the olive branch!"

"Go find another branch!"

Losing his peace, Turtle turned turtle and bit off her claw. She flew off screaching, leaving a claw taste in Turtle's mouth.

Bitter is the taste of hate ... and peace is a verb, not a noun.

Have a dovely day!

A forest of fists flew up and a triumphant bellow arose from the glowering gloom as a fighter hit the mat. He twitched and became still.

The referee held the prowling opponent back and wondered how he'd come to inhabit a world salivating over the death of careers, reputations, relationships and bodies.

He held back vomit then sighed as the twitching restarted. The prone fighter smiled his last smile as his opponent knelt, smiled and pummelled.

They pulled the referee away as two prone fighters smiled their last smiles.

Violence consumes itself and grows ever more swollen.

The cloud sat, unmoving, as if needing a visa to move on.

It cloaked us with an eerie chill we couldn't define or resist. We slowed, uncertain, shrugged, walked on, hoping safety was nearby. It didn't feel like it.

None knew the way and the confident were the less certain. Some were sure the destination was behind us, many times.

We stumbled on, hoping movement would suffice for direction and were blinded by a sudden flash.

We had escaped the cloud of life and arrived – by chance and clamour – at its certain end; right where we started.

Despite attempts to follow our bliss, change our lives and our world, we continue to re-experience the blinding mundanity from which we desire escape. We continue to wake to the numb terror, the dull regret of a life wasted and a world threatening.

A parent abused me so I distrust all authority figures. A woman embarrassed me so I distrust all women.

Only when we release past attachments to misery will a pristine new world arise before me ... a world that was always there!

I attach to the past in order to avoid a new future.

Jindalee and Dingle decided to find their father. Jindalee was excited and Dingle wasn't.

"What if he still doesn't want us?" asked Dingle.

"He's our father. He'll want to know us."

"But why did he abandon us? He must hate us."

"Let's not make up a story until we meet him," said Jindalee, masking her apprehension.

"He might beat us. Abandon us again." Dingle shivered.

"So let's spend the rest of our lives wondering, huh?"

"You ran away. I'm so glad to have you back!" boomed God's voice as he enfolded them and they all wept happily.

When you're looking down the barrel of death, waiting for destiny's trigger-pull, most concerns disappear and new thoughts emerge:

To hell with family obligations; friends get to be here by being friends, not by being from a certain sperm or egg.

Work can wait. Coffee's ready, the sun's shining and this good book is all I need right now.

What was the big deal with my health concerns? Enough of my body works to appreciate birdsong and friends' smiles. I'm just fine.

The past's dissolved (along with regret), future's a fantasy and now is all there is.

If all the world dissolved into a single idea it might be that none of this is real and Reality smiles beyond our reach.

Not a single idea in this world – in economics, science, relationships, politics, religion or any other arena of strained thinking – remains uncontested.

The experts and authorities we look up to remain on their pedestals for little more than an eye-blink before they're toppled for another.

Knowing we know nothing is the only incontestable idea we've ever had if we can but release the illusion we have any control over anything.

None at all.

Undoing the laces of her life,
Jacinta expected to find peace.
She stopped working, slept in
more, didn't answer her mobile,
socialised less, stopped needlessly
agreeing with people, pulled back on
family commitments, cancelled her
daily newspaper and paid television.
She watched the videos she chose
and read the books she chose.
In the escape, peace eluded her.
She woke earlier, planned more and
the new drum beat started.
Her laces tightened for there
was more running – in giving up
her solicitor job (and its trappings)
her franticness moved to her new
passion.
She simply switched obsessions.

From the safe stand, Patricia could recite every Wimbledon winner since 1963. She had opinions on all the contestants, scores, coaches and affairs. Each day she'd return to her tiny rented flat.

From the exciting court, Patrick only knew the players he'd shaken hands with and battled. Without opinions, he enjoyed them and the game. He remembered few of his scores and all of the risks and injuries he'd endured. He'd lost more than he'd won but, somehow, made it to the top with fortune and fame.

Are you a player or a spectator in your life?

Michael's club foot brought on ridicule and that drove him to the secret places, the lonely places.

Without friends, he had no need of a mobile for phoning, texting and Facebook. His parents left him to wander, cry, and to fester in his rage. They left him to observe, undiverted. From a wooded hilltop, he watched them searching for clues.

One time a constable briefly noticed blood on Michael's cuff but was then distracted by a text that had to be answered.

In the distractions of technology, the murderer went free and Michael was ridiculed no more.

"He's a buffoon," I exclaimed.

"Are you?" asked Karesh.

"Not me. Him. He's stupid, fickle."

"You detest your stupidity and fickleness?"

"No, I'm fine. He lies."

"You fear your lies?"

"You're not listening, Karesh. It's about him!"

"Nothing is about him. It's always about you."

"I'm fine ..."

"Yes, you're perfect. God sees you as Love." I waited, annoyed. "You're pretending that you're detestable. You hate yourself so project it to others."

"They are detestable!"

"Only when you detest yourself. Choose Love inside and you'll see only Love out there."

I wondered how God saw my Love.

Reason dances next to insanity
in the ballroom of my mind.
Each has its attendant moves
and consequences and none is as
dissimilar as I'd like to imagine.
Reason strides out in gentle waltz,
quickly interrupted by insanity's
frenetic tango, quieted by reason's
studied fox trot, soon replaced by
insanity's flailing flamenco.
Split-second choices invite
each their turn as unexpected
circumstances bite into my day's
inconstant happenstance. I am
neither reasonable nor insane, like
every fellow earth-dancer.
The defining of one or another
is only done by the truly insane,
the pretenders to reason, logic and
science.

As Dawn let slip her soft, black gown, revealing one rising orb, I cradled the shy day in my palms and asked, "How may I serve?"

There was no reply but the orb rose, casting its burnt orange glow upon the incandescent darkness. One short spread of light to soon return to its bed of night. One day too quickly be no more.

I listened again and it asked nothing but to rest in gratitude that light and dark are always with me – warm and cool, known and unknown – and my smile melded them together as one.

We arrived in Australia in boats, in chains – criminals, unwanted, uneducated and poor.

In anger and shame we stole their billions of acres and killed hundreds of thousands, hunting them for fun as we did rabbits and foxes in England. We destroyed their language, culture and spirit, raped their women and stole their children because we were better than them.

Years later, in anger and shame, we imprison the boat people who come without chains, without crimes and with qualifications and compassion. We allow women to be raped and children to die because we're better than them.

Belief and doubt – two sides to the same coin – require constant mental strain, proving something is right or not.

Hope – Holding Only Past Expectations – can but lead to anger and depression as we plant our solid staff into the sinking sands of life.

However, knowing allows us relaxation in the warm, strong hands of a greater, unmoving Truth. Releasing ourselves from the pretence of control, from the myth of intelligence, a deeper stream arises, cleansing our souls.

Nothing needs to be defended, fought for or denied. All that is left is a quiet justice ... just is.

On a street seat, watching people passing by, I wonder how scared, intrigued or amazed they are by the miracle of their birth, growth, recovery from setbacks and ability to be creative.

Many someones had to invent the idea of this street seat. Many built, painted, assembled and planted it here and here it stays – strong, comfortable and unmoved by floods, hail, blistering sun and hundreds of bums.

Does this seat's existence – the result of creativity by dozens of people we'll never know – scare, intrigue or amaze you?

Not fear but intrigue and amazement – they're my choices.

Seventeen years was all Kalban lived, what he decided to experience.

"What a waste," they said. "A coward. If only he'd done this or that ... listened to this advice. It's not right. He shouldn't, shouldn't, shouldn't ..."

The contrary, unpopular view sees that Kalban didn't waste a minute. A constant smile, a constantly helping hand, his school grades were adequate and his mountaineering feats were fantastic ... terrifying.

Do we pack in experience and choose our death or do we tread water as life's flotsam till death chooses us?

What's the biggest waste, the worst *shouldn't*?

Fear echoes not; just a black
shadow into a well of indifference.
We parade our anger and injustice
but no one's listening; no one's
repeating that tune. The fearful
imagine their posturing is heard
above the clamour of victimhood,
their Calls for Love unremembered.

Calls of Love, however, rebound
off the walls of time, sending out
their witnesses to amplify the sweet
quietude. The Love's silence is heard
in the stillness and repeated down
the river of life. The walls of fear
are split by that quiet stillness, that
remembering of oneness, and none
forget the peace.

The problem with our problems is that they're not big enough.

While arguing with neighbours over not mowing his lawn, our boss for keeping us five minutes too late or our spouse for not putting a cup in the dishwasher, our lives shrink to the size of these problems.

However, if we create massive, unforgettable problems, like creating worldwide unity and peace – as Jesus, Nelson Mandela, Martin Luther King and Mahatma Gandhi did – our lives will expand to the size of theirs.

There's always problems so let us create massive, unsolvable ones … and massive unforgettable lives.

She shrugged off her crumpled wedding dress and angrily tossed it over a chair, white and lifeless.

"Callous sod!" she whined at the mirror, her red eyes glaring back, mascara running black. "Last minute back-out! Dreams broken in one cowardly text!"

She spun round, snatched up her dress, knocking the cushion off the chair. Four money bags stared up at her, their contents spilling out. She snatched one up, quickly counted $250,000 and smiled bitterly.

She didn't notice the FBI cars screeching up to the hotel entrance as she drove off thinking, "Thank God for broken dreams!"

Filled with glamor, intrigue and danger, we thought Mogranna was a super spy, an accomplished hit-woman or the most secret of Russia's double-agents.

Behind the fur coat, spiky heels and flamboyant stories lived a sad and quiet woman who dreamed of something bigger.

She hoped big stories brought her up but they weighed her down to smallness. Her friends told her to bring her stories down to her life and then she could live past them but, by now, they'd grown past the point of a graceful landing. She crashed, dying from regret – story overload, life underlived.

He consulted with Viktor Frankl for, as a bachelor at 43, he was heartily sick of the debilitating embarrassment he felt at social occasions, especially with women.

Frankl suggested he'd continually pushed his embarrassment away and still more it came. Frankl's alternative was logical and counter intuitive but he was out of options.

The next soirée he breathed embarrassment into every cell and pore, forcing it to arise ... but it would not.[8]

In denial, the beast looms and devours. Under of the spotlight of our demands, though, it shrinks and returns to the mirage it is.

As God slept, Hermovian snuck in, quiet as a cloud, to steal God's wisdom.

He immersed his hands in the stream of wisdom, diverting them to a huge paper bag. He carried the full bag home, light as a smile.

He squashed the thoughts to fit into his mind but they wouldn't compress. He melted the thoughts down and swallowed the small, heavy blob of lead they had become. He felt smaller, heavier, and trapped. He vomited the thoughts up and felt lighter.

Returning the thoughts to God, he finally smiled again. He was free, like God.

We weakly wish for peace and furiously fight for war; then wonder why the latter invades our lives at every opportunity.

We celebrate the killing (war) and the killers (soldiers) with annual rallies, services and awards. We mourn the losses we incurred with deep, lasting sorrow and continue to send more killers out to be killed. Yet the peaceful moments get not a mention.

For centuries we remember the fallen, the crippled and the aggression. Yet we don't remember yesterday's quiet moment with a friend.

Whatever we stare at stares right back at us, every single time.

A rock is a rock is a rock and a rose is not a rose by another name. The more senses we know something by, the less names we have for it. More tangibility suggests more certainty and one name suffices.

The undetectable God, though, is known by a thousand names, a thousand natures.

Desperate to know the unknowable, we pretend to control our uncontrollable God/selves. We create a myriad of names and natures, telling us about ourselves, not God. Would not acceptance of unknowing release our prejudices and unmask the real nature of God, of ourselves?

"Our mission is not to improve ourselves," said Laslov. "We are not here to find Love, enlightenment or God's Grace."

"We do not clean our teeth to make them clean. We clean them to remove the dirt and to reveal the already clean teeth beneath.

"We know as much of God as does an unborn child knows of the world. We cannot hit a target we cannot see. We do not know Love and so our mission is to find the barriers to reveal Love. It's an unglamorous, tedious, daily duty to say, 'Let me remove this grievance so I can see the light'."

Jotesch was the wisest guru I knew ... anyone could know.

He could talk on any subject he was asked about, for hours and he could touch hearts and minds deeply.

I was happy to pay him for he gave my fuddled mind clarity and my life wings ... till the huge pedestal I'd placed him on began to crumble.

He was arrested for fraud. Then we realised that the women he was having private sessions with were not there for their counselling.

Like a compass, he always pointed north but never moved any closer to it.

Satchyn was a bullet on a mission and nothing was to stand in the way of his desires.

He knew the rules of the game and dutifully married and fathered two boys. He smiled and pretended well that he cared, while feverishly making money, fame and a difference.

His family accepted the stranger in their house for he provided all the riches a person could crave. He came and went on his clandestine missions, his money and fame growing, while building a huge store of indifference.

A heart attack at forty three and three attended his funeral.

The saver of lives, he arrived just too late. Then, realising his ambulance was full of junk, asked if he could store her husband in the house or in the shed till he came back.

"Absolutely not!" she said.

A solution presented itself and so he belted the body into the passenger seat and headed off for the hospital while his silent, wobbling friend enjoyed the view.

Having to stop several times, he chanced upon several friends who each suggested, "Your mate doesn't look too good."

He resisted saying they wouldn't look good wearing death's pallor, either![9]

Ib'n asked, "You think you hold the match that lights the sun?"

"Gosh no," I said.

"But you think you think your thoughts?"

"Well … yes."

"When two think the same thought, who's thinking it?"

"Uummm …"

"When you think of something when your mind's far away?"

"Not sure."

"All thoughts ever had or will be are present now. There is simply the releasing of prejudices, opinions and righteousness."

"Really?"

"There is no thinking, only openness. Just move out of our way, open the door and in they come."

"You think so?" I asked, cheekily.

Ib'n smiled. [10]

Miscrea, looked misty and lost. "God told me he was an atheist," she said. "I didn't know what to think or say but God looked serious; quite serious."

I wanted to make something of this; something deep and fulsome. Unsure, I made a wild guess to keep the conversation going.

"Perhaps he wants us to forget him and look to ourselves for the peace he'd give," I ventured.

"Maybe he was joking," said Miscrea, grimacing.

"Maybe you're joking."

"Maybe I don't believe in myself and he's just a mirror."

"We made God in our own image?"

"Mmm."

Happiness is general, ingrained; unhappiness is specific, outblamed.

They came to stay.

"Why are you happy, Meisje?" I asked.

"I guess I just like to be, Grandad. It's easier to be happy." She smiled and hugged me, our connection warming my heart.

"Why are you unhappy, Jongen?" I asked.

"Rains too much, sun's too hot, bed's hard, birds too loud, dog smells, food's different, mud's ..."

I thanked him and he slumped off, moaning that I didn't listen to him, the cold of separation chilling my bones.

Two ends of a magnet – one attracting, the other repelling.

The son of disappointment, Kerlin knew the bite of his mother's tongue and hand from birth. His sister, an ardent student of her mother, added her invective at him.

Kerlin's subconscious found him abusive partners till, at forty, he silently yelled, "Enough! No more scathing women!"

Then, for three years, he bathed in Marinka's sweet, gentle support, his homesickness for abuse temporarily at bay ... till it broke his resolve and he needed reconnection with the familiar discomfort of his abusive ex-partner.

Marinka was distraught and soon realised *home* may not be comfortable but it's always home.[11]

To miss someone is to remain in the hope that they will return. The fragility of hope remains even while we know they cannot and will not return, even from the grave.

Our hope to reunite creates a story of rejoining in some mythical realm where we'll never be parted again.

We wish not to be diminished by the brevity of our lives and we add gravity by creating the dream that we'll be around forever.

These dreams and stories come not from any certain knowing but from the desperation to create eternal from what will perish.

Our constant need for comfort is fuel to fire our addictions.

We're uncomfortable in this dismal, insane world; we don't fit and we yearn for that unattainable *at home* feeling.

Since we left our home in God and took up decaying carcases, we've felt guilt and despair at leaving. Neither will leave till we return.

Rather than sitting with discomfort, we try masking it – drugs, alcohol, sex, work, exercise, gossip, judgement, sickness, drama … anything.

If we could settle into knowing we'll always be uncomfortable and stay with it, would we be less naively grasping? Less addicted?

"I want my books published in at least 25 languages," I said.

"Why do you want that?" asked Sergov.

"No reason. I just do."

"You must have a reason why you want to write. Why you want to be published. Why 25."

"See that mountain?" I said.

"Yes."

"It has no reason for being there; it just is. It's immovable. That with a reason is movable, fickle even. What's unreasonable – our hearts' desires, our attractions – are inexplicable and, therefore, unmovable."

"Everything has a reason, Nikita. Everything."

"Try being unreasonable, just once," I said, but he was unmoved.

I'm a calm woman, despite the pummelling – years in hospital, foster homes and rape, teasing for my crooked walk at school, exclusion and joblessness for my wonky body and the search for acceptance in drugs, alcohol and sex. I boiled inside and flailed at people but none would listen ... till I stopped and listened to me, to God.

Somehow, the rage wore out, rubbed thin by overuse. Stillness and peace became new friends and the world lost significance.

This is no religion, this is presence. This is nought but gratitude for the choice to be grateful.

Stabbed to the bed with a searing headache, rasping throat, brittle joints and no appetite, my brain screamed while my mind took flight.

If I could be immobilised one day and active another, what's the difference? I'd just got a cold. Could I have said no to it? Could I say no now?

I imagined saying no and saw it slinking off while I leapt joyously and fitfully into a day of happy activity.

I imagined and it happened. Breathless from my jog, I'm now tucking into a hearty breakfast while I write this story to you.

You have never been before and you will never come again. This is the moment you were meant to be here because you are.

There's blame, regret, sadness and anger … they're part of you that's supposed to be here now.

The trick, Earth Voyager, is being still and listening. There's a voice without sound, a presence without form, inside you, moving you.

Of all the voices, this quietest of them is the master; the one who knows you best. This one never leaves your heart uncertain and your hands fumbling.

Relax. Listen. Smile. All is well.

Laurie, a lapsed Catholic, said, belligerently, "Spirituality is a connection, a relationship, with God. Religion is crowd control."

"Maybe," answered Friar Truck. "My take is that *religion* is derived from the Latin, *religio*, which meant reverence for God, piety. Cicero further derived it to mean *diligence*."

"If a connection comes from my reverence and diligence to God, I can have that relationship wherever I am – driving my lorry, talking with you, reading my kid a story. It's personal, not organisational."

"Perhaps."

"Then is *organised religion* a contradiction in terms?"

"Mmm, I see what you're driving at, Laurie."

I asked Garfur, the releaser of thoughts I never knew I had: "Feminists say God is female."

"And?"

"My bible says male."

"And?"

"Some say he's kind, giving. But my priest says he's wrathful, judgemental."

"And?"

"Sometimes I feel him inside me but some religions say he's out there, separate."

"And?"

"I wonder if they're all wrong ... that God's not a person ... that we made him in our own image."

"And?"

"When I still my mind and listen, it feels like God's a system, a method, to remind me of who I am."

"Your question?"

Singmax, my fine old friend from the *School of Don't Waste Life*, fielded my question: "Why doesn't *The Secret* work?"

"Huh?" she asked.

"I've made vision boards, affirmations, prayers and demands to The Universe and got less than nothing."

"Huh?"

"I asked for money and lost it, as with relationships and freedom."

"Asking brings, first, the blocks to those things. You want money, you find your negative thoughts about money, which pushes it away, till you listen and change your thoughts. Then it comes."

"I was sold a dud?"

"You were sold a quarter of a miracle."

After the frenzied rush to the abyss, there's only gut-sucking fall to oblivion; not knowing how or where I'll fall.

In the weeks before, there's crazy role changes, conflicting announcements, denials and whispered gossiping in every corner, from boardroom to toilets.

When *R Day* comes, as it must, our silent groups receive options: work part-time, apply for new jobs – some our own – or take redundancy.

Three days to decide, apply and interview and now I'm the last bus home in the rain – cold, alone and nothing to do but await others' decisions.

My future, their hands. Emptiness.

Toebuoy soon discovered that anger's expression did not diminish it. Each verbal and physical rage of his father ignited the next to greater heights, so he took his own to the quiet places.

But suppression worked no better as he hid his incendiary rage behind wide smiles and kind words.

It took Diamenta, his relentlessly caring lover, to open him to the possibility that they arrived via disappointment – unmet expectations – and so must be similarly dealt with at the mind level.

Change expectations, release judgement, change mind and release himself from the need to control. Forgiveness healed.

Life's highway of tar-seal (blacktop) turns to dust then to gold-dust …

Ensconced in a safe, lucrative job, I decide to borrow thousands for knee surgery. Then, a week before seeing the surgeon, my safe job is gone – redundancy.

Along with the crushing feelings of rejection and unworthiness, is the financial uncertainty – do I have the surgery after all?

Two days later I have a new, similar job and life continues seamlessly … now with my previous employer's redundancy gift – double the knee surgery cost!

No loan and a holiday to boot.

Life turns on two dimes!

A student of the School of Ponderingtheuniverse, Diaphenda, said, "It's like a nylon stocking."

"What is?" I asked, bemused.

"Life."

"Life?"

"It's like we're in some gigantic nylon stocking. We're all pushing and stretching but we can't get out."

"We can't?"

"We act like we have freedom but it's controlled within this invisible stocking. Also, every movement made by anyone affects everyone else so we're constrained by people and the universal stocking."

"Sounds pessimistic, limiting," I said, apprehensively.

"No, just realistic," she said and cursed. Her stocking had laddered. Her toe popped out.

We laughed freely, limitlessly.

BREAKTHROUGH

Jacqueline asked what comes before a breakthrough, the sudden realisation of a long-held dream.

"Excitement?" I asked, knowing the answer.

"What comes just before a sudden accident then?"

"Not sure," I said, hesitant.

"Exactly the same thing – nothing," she said, with a cheeky smile.

"Rubbish!" I exclaimed, thinking they had to be different.

"So tell me what comes before a breakthrough."

"Well, you must know something."

"You know nothing beyond that you've been watering and fertilizing your dream with regular action since you dreamt it."

"You never know when it's coming?"

"Nope. Never. You just keep watering."

The end of all things must come in this illusion, my friend – relationships, health, careers, toys. Everything.

Nothing is to be relied on for everything decays. Nothing. But this illusion is not our home.

We came for a moment in time to experience time's limitations. We came to know of separation, loneliness, judgement and transience. Ah, blessed transience to which we cling in our temporary insanity!

We can, however, wake and forgive our insane attachments. We can, in a blip, change our minds and return home to limitlessness, acceptance, peace and joy … if we wish to.

Appendix

1. Front cover - The Language Labyrinth is at: https://web.facebook.com/thelanguagelabyrinth/
2. Page 23 - Each year 100-200 million sharks die from human attacks while 38 humans die from shark attacks.
3. Page 25 - This happened to me at Palm Beach, Gold Coast, Australia.
4. Page 39 - Quoted from *A Course in Miracles*.
5. Page 42 - A true story of farmer client of mine (when I was an accountant) kept his annual accounts in the effluent pit ... quite legally. They were never inspected.
6. Page 44 - This actually happened while eight of us were fishing in the estuary of Bribie Island, Queensland, Australia.
7. Page 47 - The quote is from *A Course in Miracles.*
8. Page 77 - A story from Victor Frankl's book, *Man's Search for Meaning.*
9. Page 84 - a true story told by my friend, Stephen Benner, of an ambulance driver in Tauranga, New Zealand.
10. Page 85 - "You think you hold the match that lights the sun?" is a quote from *A Course in Miracles*.
11. Page 88 - the true story of a friend of mine, with names and times changed.
12. The two images - pages 105 and 110 - were drawn on the whiteboard by Moci Gao, a student of mine.

Heart ...

In New Zealand I experienced life as an accountant, credit manager, company director, shepherd, scrub-cutter, tree pruner, freezing worker, plastics factory worker, saxophonist, army driver, tour bus driver, stage and television actor and singer, builder, lecturer, facilitator for men's groups, reporter, columnist, magazine editor, publisher, writer ...

In South Africa as an AIDS workshop co-facilitator ...

In the Australian bush as a barman, horse and camel trekker and stock-whip teacher ...

In England as a contract accountant, corporate trainer, estate manager, lecturer, singer/songwriter, website editor/writer and freelance writer ...

Now that I'm back in Australia, house renovating, teaching and writing, I'm wondering what's next!

The constant for my wife and I is *A Course in Miracles*, a psychological life-style course in forgiveness. Through it I have found the peace I had always been searching for - the journey to where we have always been.

Join me in social media:

Website: www.philipjbradbury.com
Shopify: https://philip-j-bradbury-books.myshopify.com/
About Me: https://about.me/philipbradbury
Amazon: amzn.to/25X0CLb
Facebook:
https://www.facebook.com/AuthorPhilipJBradbury/
Google+: http://bit.ly/2bsbpUy
Linked In - http://bit.ly/2aTzZMS
Pininterest: https://au.pinterest.com/bradburywords/
Smashwords: http://bit.ly/2aNjkic
Twitter: https://twitter.com/PhilipJBradbury
Website: www.philipjbradbury.com
Wordpress blogs:
https://flashfictionfanatic.wordpress.com/
https://pjbradbury.wordpress.com/

Other books by Philip J Bradbury

Non-Fiction
Whose Life Is It Anyway?
The Lawless Way
Change Your Life, Change Your World
The Twelve Week Miracle (with Anna Bradbury)
Understanding Men
Articles of Faith
Conversations on Your Business
Stepping Out Of Debt and Into Financial Freedom

Some-Fiction
Dactionary – the dictionary with attitude
The Meaning of Larf

Fiction
An Olympic Challenge
The Royal Bank of Stories
Circles of Gold
Gerald the Great of Gorokoland

Words in progress - looking for a publisher
40 Moments With Writing
42 Moments With Men
50 Moments With Fables
55 Moments With God
65 Moments With Self
The Last Stand-Down
The Last Accusation
The Last Expulsion

For more information on these books, see
www.philipjbradbury.com

97 SMILES

97
Special
Moments
In Life's
Exquisite
Simplicity

Philip J Bradbury

Published by The Write Site

ISBN- 978-0-9922908-4-9

Thank you ...

I am able to put these intangible ideas into words and Anna, my wife, is able to put them into action; the reason she's such a good life coach. She is my best friend and greatest inspiration and I thank her from the bottom of my beating heart for being there, for loving me and for being that which I wish for myself.

Anna edited this book with her razor eye for the details I didn't see.

Thank you also to Tracie Louise for her beautiful cover photograph. You can see more of Tracie Louise's photographs at http://tracielouise.com.

In my 1996 Business Start-Up class, a student came to learn how to help her husband set up an aviation museum. She constantly doodled through class and I took her aside after the fist lesson and asked about her real passion. It was not aviation but art and, by the 3rd of 17 lessons, she'd told her husband to set up his own museum and she eventually ran her own successful children's art school. It may still be going. The cover image is one of the "doodles" she allowed me to take home. Sadly, I've forgotten her name and if you find this book, please contact me and I'll send you a free one in deep gratitude for your fine skills and generosity.

I am also indebted to *A Course in Miracles* - and all the people I have met through it - for it shows me the way to peace; that way that is both simple and difficult. Forgiveness is simple but it's difficult to do in every second of our lives.

I keep trying ...